The Scottish Folk Fiddle Third Position Book

by
Christine Martin

Published by
Taigh na Teud (Harpstring House)

ISBN 1 871931 52 5

TAIGH NA TEUD
13 BREACAIS ARD
ISLE OF SKYE
IV42 8PY
SCOTLAND
taighnateud@martin.abel.co.uk
http://www.abel.net.uk/~martin

For a catalogue of all our publications including the "Ceilidh Collection" series,
"Ceol na Fidhle" Highland Tunes for the Fiddle and "Session Books" etc. please
contact the publishers at the address above or visit our web site.

Introduction

This book is to introduce fiddlers to the third position in a fun and exciting way by setting well known Scottish tunes as the examples. The book can be used on its own or in conjunction with one of the violin third position books on the market which specialise in classical music. Also included here are a couple of pages of second position work.

As the hand moves to third position remember to shift the thumb at the same time so it is in the same relative position in third as it was in first position. When the various techniques for position changing have been learned they can readily be applied to other positions on the fiddle.

Position changing is used not only to access more notes but also to improve tone quality and for ease of playing in some musical patterns. There are many examples of third position tunes in "Ho-ro Gheallaidh" 1 & 2 and in "Cruinn Còmhla" for you to try.

Thanks to Anne Hughes and Jean Ann Callender for their valuable suggestions and contributions to the material in this book.

Contents

Ae Fond Kiss	22	Grand Old Duke of York	4
Amazing Grace	16	Hector the Hero	21
An Coinneachan	7	The Hills of Glenorchy	15
Archibald MacDonald of Keppoch	15	The Hopeful Lover	9
Auld Lang Syne	23	Hot Cross Buns	4
Au Claire de la Lune	5	Iain Ruaridh's Lament	22
Away in a Manger	6	Jesus Hands are Kind Hands	5
Buain nan Dearcan ris an Spreidh	8	Katie Bairdie	10
The Bugle Horn	9	The Lass of Bon Accord	20
Caisteal a' Ghlinne	23	Leanaibh an Aigh	11
The Call of the Red Bird	19	Lochaber Cronan	18
Castle of the Glen	23	Loch Duich	12
Coilsfield House	24	Lovely Stornoway	7
Colin's Cattle	8	MacPherson's Rant	16
Coulters Candy	5	Morning has Broken	11
The Cradle Song	17	The Music o' Spey	20
Crodh Chailein	8	The Rowan Tree	12
Donald MacPherson's Lament	14	Skye Boat Song	24
Eilean Mo Chridhe	10	The Sweetness of Mary	14
Fairy Lullaby	7	Tuireadh Iain Ruaidh	22
The First Nowell	6	Westering Home	10
The Flower of the Quern	17	Ye Banks and Braes	11

Play open D followed by 3rd finger on A.   Then change 3rd finger to a first finger to find the
first note in these tunes and exercises

3rd position notes on the A string

Grand Old Duke of York

Hot Cross Buns

3rd position notes on the E string

Play test notes before you begin

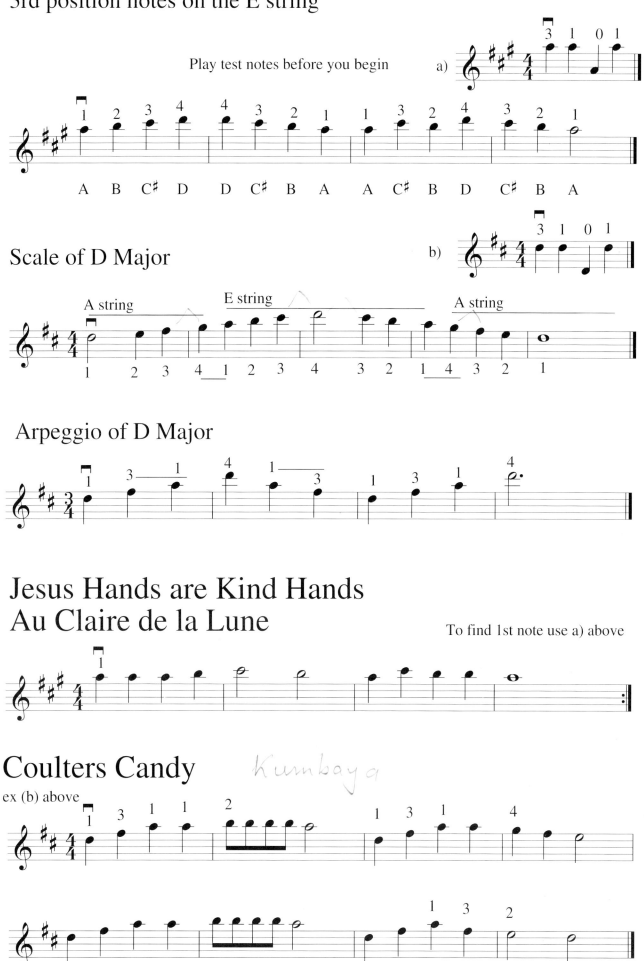

Scale of D Major

Arpeggio of D Major

Jesus Hands are Kind Hands
Au Claire de la Lune

To find 1st note use a) above

Coulters Candy

Kumbaya

ex (b) above

5

The First Nowell

Ex to help find 1st note

Move up or down between 1st and 3rd positions
as you are playing the open A string

1st pos   3rd pos

Away in a Manger

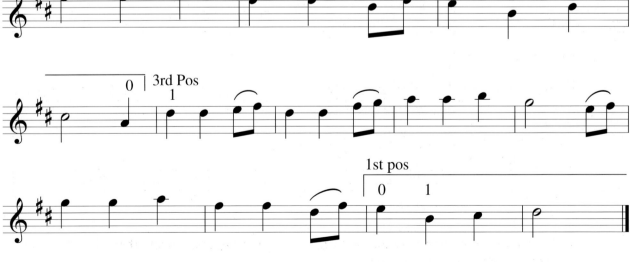

1st pos

3rd Pos

1st pos

Fairy Lullaby An Coineachan

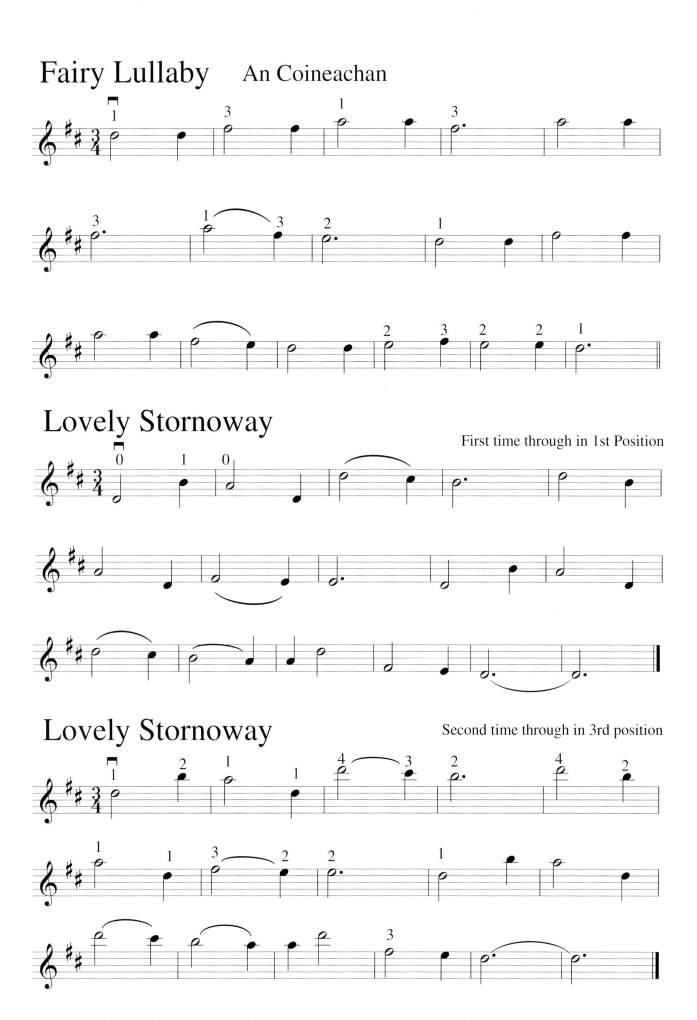

Lovely Stornoway

First time through in 1st Position

Lovely Stornoway

Second time through in 3rd position

In waltzes it is quite common to play the first time through in 1st position and then play the second time through up an octave in 3rd position.

Notes on the D string in 3rd position
G scale in 3rd Position

G A B C D E F# G G F# E D C B A G

Crodh Chailein Colin's Cattle

Buain nan Dearcan ris an Sprèidh
(Gathering the berries for the cows)

8

The Bugle Horn

3rd Pos

1st Pos

3rd Pos

Revise D scale and arpeggio on Page 5.

The Hopeful Lover

1)   C natural on the E string   2)   F natural on the A string

A   B   C♮   D   D   C♮   B   A   D   E   F♮   G   G   F♮   E   D

Eilean mo Chridhe
Westering Home

Katie Bairdie

\ lines are used in Scottish fiddle playing instead of

10

C major Scale and Arpeggio

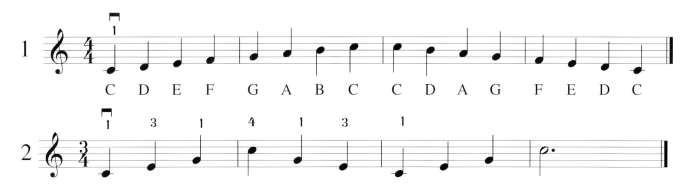

Leanaibh an Aigh

Morning has broken

Ye Banks and Braes

Slide up and down keeping thumb loose

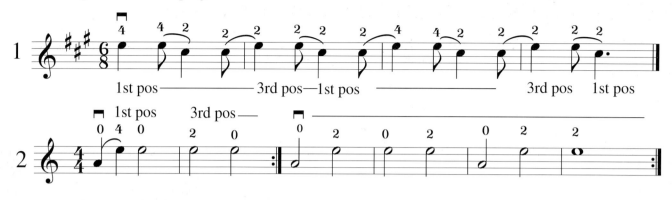

1

1st pos ——————— 3rd pos—1st pos ——————— 3rd pos   1st pos

2

1st pos   3rd pos ——

Loch Duich

1st pos

The Rowan Tree

Some useful position changing exercises

These exercises are frequently used by fiddlers when changing position. Slide fingers when changing.
When you are fluent at these exercises the stepping notes should be used but not heard.

The scale line shift

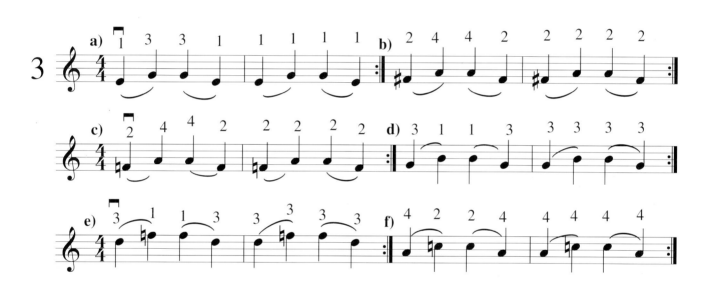

Changing position using a stepping note

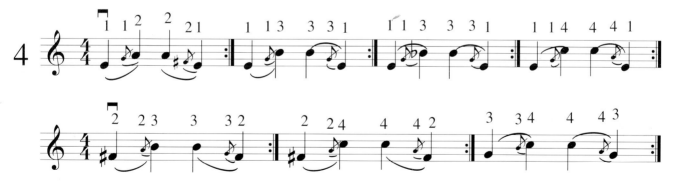

Donald McPherson's Lament

J. S. Skinner

(ex (d) p.13)

The Sweetness of Mary

Joan MacDonald Boes

Strathspey
mod. slow

The Hills of Glenorchy

Cape Breton Style

Scale of F major

Archibald MacDonald of Keppoch

15

Amazing Grace

(Could use alternative fingering in brackets and stay in 3rd position throughout)

MacPherson's Rant
Third position here allows an interesting bagpipe drone. You can practise the position changes first without the drone.

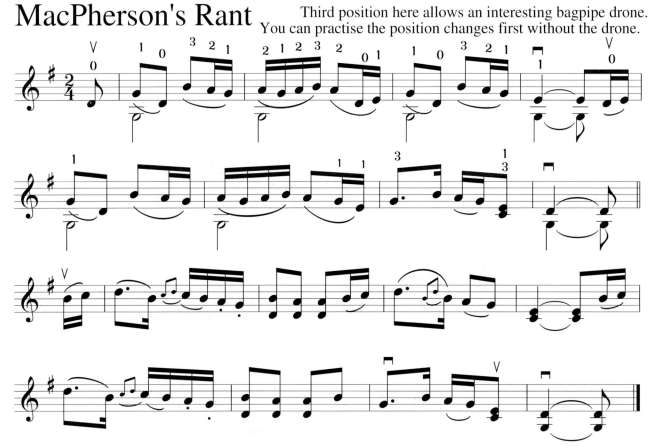

Twinkle Twinkle

The Cradle Song

J. Scott Skinner

The Flower of the Quern

J.Scott Skinner

Harmonics- There are two kinds of harmonics which can be played on the violin. Natural harmonics which are shown here and artificial harmonics. Natural harmonics are played at the halfway point on the string with the little finger.
Extend the little finger so it touches the string lightly and it produces a bell like sound.

Harmonics

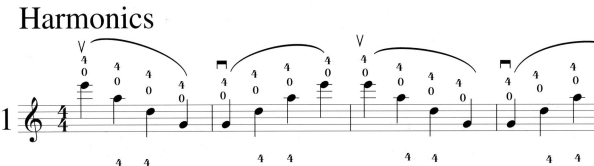

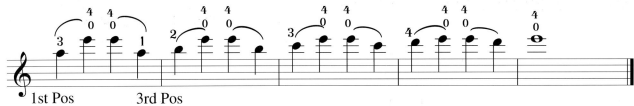

American Theme

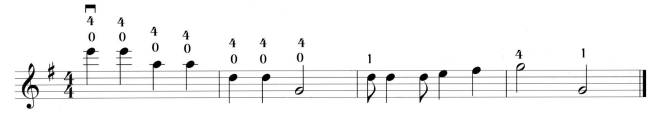

Lochaber Cronan

D.C. al Fine

18

The Call of the Red Bird

Jubal Anderson

+ = L.H. Pizz

19

The Music o' Spey

J. Scott Skinner

The Lass of Bon Accord

20

Hector the Hero

Revise Ex b) on page 20

Some tunes are more easily played in 2nd position so here are a few examples to try.

Scale of F major and Arpeggio in 2nd Position

Tuireadh Iain Ruaidh

Iain Ruairidh's Lament

Ae Fond Kiss

Caisteal a' Ghlinne Castle of the Glen

Auld Lang Syne

C Major Scale

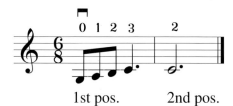

1st pos.   2nd pos.

Skye Boat Song

Fine

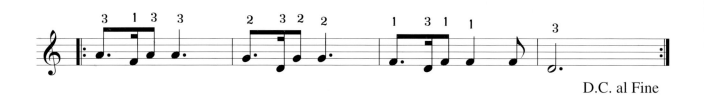

D.C. al Fine

Coilsfield House

(This tune uses 1st, 2nd and 3rd positions)

Nathanial Gow